The Library of Author Biographies™

M. E. Kerr

The Library of Author Biographies ™

M. E. KERR

Albert Spring

The Rosen Publishing Group, Inc., New York

To A.L.S. and J.L.S.

Published in 2006 by The Rosen Publishing Group, Inc.
29 East 21st Street, New York, NY 10010

First Edition

Library of Congress Cataloging-in-Publication Data

Spring, Albert.
M. E. Kerr / Albert Spring.—1st ed.
  p. cm.—(The library of author biographies)
Includes bibliographical references and index.
ISBN 1-4042-0465-2 (lib. bdg.)
1. Kerr, M. E. 2. Novelists, American—20th century—Biography.
3. Young adult fiction—Authorship. I. Title. II. Series.
PS3561.E643Z86 2006
813'.54—dc22

                                    2004024942

Manufactured in the United States of America

The *Horn Book Magazine*, September/October 1986. Text reprinted by permission of The Horn Book, Inc., Boston, MA, www.hbook.com.

The *Horn Book Magazine*, June 1977. Text reprinted by permission of The Horn Book, Inc., Boston, MA, www.hbook.com.

Text from *Presenting M. E. Kerr*, by Alleen Pace Nilsen, Twayne Publishers, ©1986, Twayne Publishers. Reprinted by permission of The Gale Group.

Text from *Booklist*, Sept. 15, 1994. Used with permission. Copyright © American Library Association.

Table of Contents

Introduction:
Not Like the Others

M. E. Kerr is one of the most widely read and critically acclaimed writers of young adult fiction in North America. She is also one of its pioneers. When she began writing literature for and about teens in the early 1970s, she was one of a handful of talented writers including S. E. Hinton (*The Outsiders*, 1967), Paul Zindel (*The Pigman*, 1968), Robert Lipsyte (*The Contender*, 1967), Richard Peck (*Don't Look and It Won't Hurt*, 1972), Paula Fox (*The Slave Dancer*, 1973), Norma Fox Mazer (*A Figure of Speech*, 1973), and Robert Cormier (*The Chocolate War*, 1974). These authors were intent on tackling tough issues such as prejudice, sexuality, divorce, and death. At the time, these

7

topics were viewed as inappropriate subject matter for young people.

In her novels, Kerr focuses on teenagers with real or imagined differences—outsiders who are often loners. Her characters are the type of young people who are most likely to pick up a novel and look for refuge within its pages. In fact, they are quite similar to how Kerr herself was as a teenager. In a recent interview, Kerr describes how she was as a young girl:

> I was a bookworm and a poetry lover. When I think of myself and what I would have liked to have found in books those many years ago, I remember being depressed by all the neatly tied-up, happy-ending stories, the abundance of winners, the themes of winning, solving, finding—when around me it didn't seem that easy.[1]

Kerr's career as a young adult (YA) author is quite uncommon. When she wrote her first novel for teens, *Dinky Hocker Shoots Smack!* (1972), she was forty-five years old and had been making a living as an adult novelist for more than twenty years. Of course, few people knew this about M. E. Kerr. This is because the name M. E. Kerr only came into being while the author was at work on *Dinky Hocker*. This new pseudonym was but one of a list of pen names she had been writing under since she first began sending out stories to publishers as a teenager.

M. E. Kerr has proved to be a lucky name. Since the publication of her first YA novel, Kerr has met with enormous success with critics, teachers, librarians, parents, and readers of all ages. Writing about intelligent outsiders with serious problems in dynamic prose that combines realism with large doses of humor, she has carved out an important place in the field of young adult literature.

1 Growing Up

Marijane Agnes Meaker—M. E. Kerr—was born on May 27, 1927, in the town of Auburn, New York. The middle child of Ellis and Ida Meaker, Marijane had two brothers. However, the age difference between them was so great that she sometimes felt as if she were an only child. Marijane was only twelve when her older brother moved away from home. During the same year, her younger brother was born.

Ellis and Ida Meaker

Marijane's father, Ellis, was quite a character. He had fought with the French army during World War I (1914–1918). Nostalgic for his days in France, when he returned to the United States, he took to wearing a beret when he rode around town on his bicycle. In doing so, he resembled the typical Frenchmen from small towns he had encountered overseas. In Auburn, Ellis made his living manufacturing mayonnaise until World War II broke out in 1939. With the war on, trade with Europe was cut off. This led to a shortage of many essential foods in the United States. Unlike sugar, butter, and onions, mayonnaise was not considered an essential product. Accordingly, during the war years, Ellis's factory switched to making dehydrated onions.

Young Marijane was embarrassed by the fact that her hometown reeked of onions. Even her father was embarrassed. To make the townspeople aware of the importance of his onion business, he placed ads in the local paper stating: "Our onions are for field rations for our fighting men. When you smell onions, pray for peace."[1]

In his spare time, Ellis loved reading everything from classic literature to popular magazines such as *Time* and *Life*. All four walls of the Meaker living room were lined with overflowing bookshelves. Young Marijane acquired her passion for reading from her father. From an early age, she loved nothing more than to sit in her room, devouring books. She was fascinated by the stories themselves, as well as the authors who wrote them. Like many children who dream of becoming movie stars, Marijane can't remember a time when she didn't long to be a writer. Her love of literature also developed into a love of libraries. Passionate about history, Ellis frequently went to the local library to do research. Marijane often accompanied him on these trips and spent long hours happily browsing through the stacks.

Her passion for reading was accompanied by a desire to write. Ellis kept a journal and encouraged his daughter to keep one as well. He gave her a diary and instructed her to write down her thoughts and observations. Years later, these diary entries would prove essential for M. E. Kerr the writer—they helped her remember in detail what it was like to be young.

Thanks to her mother, Ida, Marijane found lots of things to write about in her diary. Ida was not only an obsessive people-watcher, but she was also a serious snoop. When Ida Meaker visited friends, she regularly looked through their bathroom cabinets to discover what medicines they were taking. On Saturday evenings, accompanied by Marijane, Ida would drive downtown and park the car. Although she would pull out her knitting needles and a ball of yarn, Ida actually spent more time spying on people. She would comment to Marijane about who was entering the cinema with whom and which men were drinking at the bar. On the way home, she would comment on whose house needed to be painted and whose car was parked in front of whose driveway. Because of these outings, Marijane became a careful observer of details—a useful talent for a future writer.

A Tomboy

As a young girl, Marijane preferred to play with boys rather than girls. She also liked to dress like a boy. She loved wearing her older brother's outgrown shirts and pants as well as vests from her father's business suits. As she entered her teens, however, her mother began to worry that her daughter's tomboy ways were preventing her from becoming popular.

Hoping to increase Marijane's chances at popularity by making her graceful and ladylike, when Marijane turned thirteen, Ida Meaker enrolled her daughter in Laura Bryan's school for ballroom dancing. Week after week, Marijane spent an hour gliding around the dance floor with an unpopular boy named Clinton Klock. After class, most boys asked their partners to go out for a soda at Miss

Margaret's ice-cream parlor. However, Clinton never invited Marijane. Mrs. Meaker couldn't understand why. She pestered Marijane so much that Marijane decided that she would ask Clinton to go out for a soda. When he declined, saying he was saving all his money to buy a boat, Marijane offered to pay for him. When Clinton confessed to his mother that Marijane had treated him to a soda, and Mrs. Klock in turn told Ida Meaker, Marijane was so embarrassed that she almost threw up. She had never felt like such a loser. Back in the 1940s, it was unheard of for a girl to treat a boy; men were always expected to pay.

Boarding School

In 1943, Marijane's parents sent her to Stuart Hall, a boarding school in Virginia. She was sixteen years old. During her first semester, she was assigned to live with Kay Walters, the first preacher's daughter she had ever met. The following semester, she was moved into a room with a deaf girl named Agnes Thatcher, the first handicapped person she had ever known. Both experiences gave her insights into what it is like to be different, to be treated as an outsider because of one's religion or physical disabilities.

At school, Marijane began writing short stories, which she sent off to magazines. Most of these were romantic tales with sad endings. The summer between her junior and senior years, seventeen-year-old Marijane came home to Auburn to discover that her parents had bought a summer cottage on a lake far away from town. One of the reasons they had done so was because Auburn was full of sailors from a nearby naval base. Protective of his daughter, Ellis Meaker didn't want Marijane anywhere near so many young men on the loose. He had heard too many stories of sailors seducing young women and getting them pregnant.

Isolated at the cottage, Marijane took care of her younger brother and spent a lot of time writing stories that she sent off to magazines. In return, the magazines sent her rejection slips. One letter she received described a story of hers as "touching." Marijane was so thrilled by this praise that for weeks she carried the slip around in the back pocket of her jeans.

Eventually, Ida Meaker became worried about her daughter being cooped up in a bedroom all the time, writing. She complained to Ellis that Marijane was becoming antisocial. Finally, Ellis agreed that Marijane could get a job in town. He even bought her a secondhand convertible because there was no bus service between the cottage and Auburn.

Eavesdropping

Marijane adored both her car and her job as an operator at the telephone company. Although all she did was sit in front of a switchboard pushing plugs and saying "Number please?" she soon discovered how to listen to conversations. She eavesdropped on her girlfriends gossiping. She also listened in on her mother telling her friends about life in the Meaker family.

Some of the things Marijane discovered surprised her. For instance, she had no idea that her mother suspected her father was having an affair with his secretary. She also never knew that Ida had become pregnant with her little brother in order to keep Ellis involved in family life. Moreover, she was surprised to discover why her mother thought Marijane spent so much time writing. Ida confessed to a friend that she thought Marijane was self-conscious about her long nose and assumed that writing was her way of hiding from the world. In truth, until she eavesdropped on her mother, Marijane had never thought anything was wrong with her nose. Now, suddenly, she did.

"Haves" and "Have-Nots"

That summer promised to become more exciting when a friend from school arrived for a visit.

Perhaps because she didn't have many friends to begin with, Marijane considered Jan Fox to be the most sophisticated girl she'd ever met in her life. She was impressed by the fact that Jan had wealthy parents, drank martinis, and smoked cigarettes. At the same time, Marijane was ashamed of her own middle-class family, whom she suddenly viewed as hopelessly unsophisticated. She even warned her parents not to act too small-town.

However, when Jan arrived, Marijane became terribly ashamed of the Meakers' simple summer cottage, the baked beans her mother served for dinner, and the fact that there was no cocktail hour at 5 PM. Even worse was when two young men showed up to take Jan and Marijane out on dates. Marijane's overprotective father insisted that both boys come inside the house to introduce themselves and show him their drivers' licenses. Marijane was so embarrassed she wanted to sink into the ground.

Ultimately, the summer provided Marijane with various learning experiences. Jan's visit forced Marijane to confront the difference between "haves" and "have-nots" (among which she included herself). This would later become a major theme in her novels. Meanwhile, she discovered how liberating it could be to create another identity for herself by using a pseudonym. Marijane signed the stories she sent off to magazines with the name Eric Ranthram McKay. The initials "E. R. M." were her father's. They were engraved on his stationery, on which she typed her stories. As Eric Ranthram McKay, Marijane Meaker realized that she could write about people she knew without them knowing who was telling their secrets. It was the beginning of a method she would use throughout her career as a writer.

Away at School

While in her last year at boarding school, Marijane got into serious trouble. During Christmas vacation in Auburn, she bought a dartboard and decorated it with photos of teachers from Stuart Hall. Beneath each picture, she wrote a rude caption. Back at school, Marijane's dartboard was a big success among her dorm mates. However, it proved less popular with the staff, one member of which discovered it in her closet. As a punishment, Marijane was expelled from school and sent home.

Back in Auburn, Marijane got a job in a local defense plant, where arms were manufactured for the war. Meanwhile, her parents wrote letters to Stuart Hall, pleading that Marijane be allowed back in so she could graduate. In April, the school agreed to readmit Marijane. She returned to finish her year.

Armed with her high school diploma, it was time to think about where to go to college. On this subject, the Meaker family was in strong disagreement. Like many Americans of his generation, Ellis Meaker thought that the main reason a woman went to university was so she could meet a good husband. Because of this, he wanted Marijane to go to Syracuse University. Located close to home, it would allow Marijane to meet a local young man who would want to marry and have kids near Auburn. Meanwhile, Marijane herself dreamed of going to the University of Missouri, which had one of the best journalism schools in the country. Ultimately, the dispute was decided by Marijane's final grades. They were so terrible that neither university accepted her. Instead, she ended up going to Vermont Junior College in the fall of 1945. There, she started the campus newspaper. As the paper's founder and editor, it was hardly surprising that Marijane herself wrote most of the articles.

During her first year, Marijane did so well in her studies that she was able to transfer to the University of Missouri. However, at the university, because she arrived last minute as a transfer student, there was no affordable housing available.

She had two options: return home to Auburn or join a sorority and move into their house. In order to become a member of a sorority, Marijane and other candidates had to endure rush week, a week-long series of humiliating activities. Although she hated the experience, in the end, she was invited to join the Alpha Delta Pi sorority.

Always somewhat of an outsider and a rebel, Marijane disliked the conformity of sorority life. Sisters (members of the sorority) were encouraged to be part of the group and dress and behave in similar fashions. Individuality and differences were frowned upon. Because of this, Marijane sought out the friendship of other journalism students and campus intellectuals. She found them to be more independent and interesting. She also enjoyed spending time with aspiring writers. They would encourage each other in their writing pursuits.

Meanwhile, Marijane continued to write and submit stories to magazines. She and her friends had a saying: never commit suicide as long as you have a manuscript in the mail. It was important to be constantly sending out stories. Even so, Marijane continued to receive rejection letters. In fact, at a sorority costume party, she showed up as a rejection slip. She wore a long black slip with actual rejection letters sent to her from magazines pinned to it.

In the summer of 1948, Marijane fell in love with a Hungarian refugee who was somewhat of a revolutionary. Influenced by him, she joined the Communist Party. She also began working as a volunteer at a local mental hospital. When her Hungarian boyfriend became too caught up in politics, she began dating the head psychiatrist at the mental hospital. Later, she dated a student majoring in English at the university who helped convince her to switch her major from journalism to English literature. Marijane was frustrated by journalism because it only dealt with facts. In contrast, writing fiction meant that she could express her own ideas and use her imagination.

2 Pseudonyms

When Marijane graduated from the University of Missouri in 1949, she did what many ambitious young American writers do: she moved to New York City. She rented an apartment with three college friends who had also moved east. In order to pay rent, she got a series of boring office jobs, none of which lasted very long. In fact, in her first year alone, she was hired and fired from nine different companies. However, throughout this period, she never stopped writing.

Eventually, her determination paid off. On April 20, 1951, twenty-three-year-old Marijane Meaker sold her first story to the magazine *Ladies' Home Journal*. At the time, this women's magazine published quality fiction by reputed female authors. Marijane was so thrilled with the sale that she misread the acceptance letter they had sent her. She thought she was getting paid $75. In reality she received $750.

Laura Winston

The story—a young adult romance set in a boarding school similar to Stuart Hall—was published under the pseudonym Laura Winston. Bruce Gould, the editor of *Ladies' Home Journal*, liked Laura's story so much that he traveled to New York to meet her agent, Marijane Meaker. He was terribly surprised when he discovered that both were the same woman.

Interested by Marijane's double role as writer/ agent, Gould arranged for her to be interviewed on the radio. As it turned out, an editor at Fawcett Publications named Dick Carroll was listening to the interview. Coincidentally, he remembered that Marijane had briefly worked at Fawcett when she had first arrived in New York. Carroll tracked down Marijane and asked her if she would like to write a book set in a boarding school. Marijane was ecstatic, but she asked if the story could take place at a sorority house, as this was a setting with which she was more familiar.

She spent the next few months writing an outline and a few sample chapters in the hope that Fawcett would purchase the story. Then Carroll came to New York to have lunch with her. On the way to the restaurant, Carroll told Marijane the good news: they liked the story and he was going to give her an advance payment of $2,000. When they came back out into the sunshine, Marijane Meaker was under contract to write her first novel.

Vin Packer

Spring Fire (1952) was based on Marijane's own experiences at a sorority house. When it was published, it was quite a sensation because it dealt with lesbianism, a subject that was not openly discussed at the time. When she was still in high school at Stuart Hall, Marijane had her first lesbian experiences. Although these were mostly limited to kissing, they were kept a secret. In the 1940s and 1950s, homosexuality was viewed by most of American society as a crime and a sin. To openly show affection for someone of the same sex was almost impossible. *Spring Fire*, however, was a great success, selling over a million copies when it came out in paperback in 1952. The novel established Marijane as a professional writer. It also provided her with a big increase in income. After taking a long-desired trip to Europe, she was able to move to an apartment of her own in Manhattan. She would live there for the next eight years.

Marijane's debut novel had been published under the pseudonym Vin Packer. The idea for a male pseudonym came from her editor at Fawcett who believed that a female writing racy suspense stories wouldn't be taken seriously by readers. Marijane chose the name Vin Packer after discussing the editor's comments over dinner with two friends, one whose first name was Vin and the other whose last name was Packer. Between 1952 and 1969, Marijane churned out twenty novels as Vin Packer. Most Vin Packer books were thrillers, and most of the protagonists were young people, often lesbians. Between 1958 and 1972, she also published five novels using the name Ann Aldrich. The main characters of these journalistic novels were all lesbians who lived in New York.

M. J. Meaker

During the 1960s, Marijane did attempt to write other kinds of books. In 1964, Doubleday commissioned her to write a nonfiction book about famous suicides. The experience was frustrating because her editor wouldn't let her insert her own ideas about why famous people such as Marilyn Monroe and

Ernest Hemingway had killed themselves. He also didn't want the book to be published under her full name, arguing that "Marijane" wasn't a suitable name for a book about suicide. In the end, *Sudden Endings* (1964) was published under the name M. J. Meaker. Three years later, M. J. Meaker also wrote what she referred to as the autobiographical family novel that every young writer must write to get out of his or her system. According to Marijane, her family novel, entitled *Hometown* (1967), was terrible. The only impact it had was in Auburn, where Marijane's embarrassed relatives busied themselves removing copies from local libraries and bookstores.

Marijane loved living in New York City. There were many interesting things to do and people to meet. Over the years, Marijane took courses at a reputed Manhattan university called the New School. Aside from creative writing, she also studied literature, anthropology, sociology, and political science. In particular, psychology interested her. She became great friends with one of her psychology professors, Martha Wolfenstein, a psychoanalyst who specialized in treating children and teens. Martha lent Marijane many books and journals about psychology. She also told her many stories about her young clients and their problems (without revealing their identities).

Marijane's friendship with Martha influenced her writing in several ways. The focus of her Vin Packer thrillers began to change. Instead of concentrating on who committed a crime, they explored the reasons why. Frequently, the main characters were young people whose emotional problems she described in great realistic detail. Another good friend of Marijane's observed her skill at portraying young people and encouraged her to write a novel for teenagers. This friend was Louise Fitzhugh, author of the highly successful children's book *Harriet the Spy* (1964).

The character of Harriet—a tough, curious, lonely tomboy—hit such a nerve with young readers that in the late 1960s, *Harriet the Spy* clubs mushroomed all over the United States. Although Marijane greatly admired Louise's book, she didn't want to limit herself by writing for a younger audience. However, she changed her mind a few years later after reading another famous book for young adults called *The Pigman*.

The author of *The Pigman*, Paul Zindel, was a playwright who, up until then, had only written for adults. Marijane was so impressed by the maturity and realism of *The Pigman*, she felt challenged to take Louise Fitzhugh's advice and try her own hand at writing a novel specifically for young

"Marijane the Spy"

Marijane remembers telling Louise Fitzhugh that when she was a child, she would roam her neighborhood in Auburn, spying on people and writing down what they did. She even had a sign up on her bedroom door: "Marijane the Spy." Louise was obviously thinking about Marijane when she sat down and wrote her first novel for young people, *Harriet the Spy*. Although the title character became one of the most popular characters in children's literature, Marijane swears that Harriet wasn't based on her but on Louise herself.

adults. But what would she write about? The idea for a novel came out of a personal experience that recently occurred to her.

Dinky Hocker

In the late 1960s, Marijane began participating as a volunteer in an experimental writers-in-the-school program. One day a month, she went to a Manhattan high school and tried to interest poor black teens in creative writing. One of the most popular writers was an overweight girl named Tiny who made up highly imaginative but grotesque stories. After reading Tiny's stories, Tiny's mother met with

Marijane to complain about her daughter's "weird" writing. Over the months, Marijane came to know a lot about Tiny. She discovered that Tiny's mother was a professional do-gooder who spent most of her time at the neighborhood church trying to help drug addicts. Tiny would come home from school to an empty apartment and sit and eat junk food in front of the television. Her mother would come home to eat dinner and then return to the church, leaving Tiny to sit alone in front of the television until she fell asleep. Marijane was struck by the fact that while the mother was solving other people's problems, her own daughter was becoming dangerously overweight and desperately unhappy.

This mother-daughter relationship became the central plot of Marijane's first novel for young adults, *Dinky Hocker Shoots Smack!* (1972). Although she changed the characters' skin color and economic background to fit the white, middle-class segment of the population with which she was more familiar, the personalities and problems remained the same.

In the novel, Tiny became Dinky Hocker. The only daughter of two liberal upper-class parents, Dinky is starved for attention but not for food. She wolfs down junk food nonstop and grows increasingly large. Dinky's father is a successful lawyer who is rarely at home. Her mother spends all her time and energy helping reform drug addicts. Tiny's only friend is Tucker Woolf, a sensitive teen from her Brooklyn Heights neighborhood. It is he who narrates the story.

Tucker sets Dinky up with P. John Knight, a "fatty" like her, with a rebellious streak that Dinky admires. The ultra-conservative P. John makes fun of every liberal cause that Dinky's parents support. Finally, the Hockers forbid Dinky to see P. John. Dinky becomes so desperate that while Mrs. Hocker is being honored at a community dinner for her work with drug addicts, Dinky paints the message "Dinky Hocker Shoots Smack!" on neighborhood walls, sidewalks, and cars. As people come out of the awards ceremony, they are shocked by what they see—and of course, so are Mr. and Mrs. Hocker.

M. E. Kerr

Marijane sent the finished manuscript of *Dinky Hocker Shoots Smack!* to Harper and Row (today HarperCollins Children's Books), the same New York publishing house that published *Harriet the Spy*. Editor Ursula Nordstrom (who also worked with Louise Fitzhugh) loved the novel and agreed to publish it. But under what name? Marijane had already used both M. J. Meaker and Marijane

Meaker for adult books. A lover of word games and double meanings, she finally came up with M. E. Kerr, a play on her last name—Meaker. She later admitted that the choice was probably a result of the belief that a female author wouldn't sell as well as a male.

The hardcover edition of M. E. Kerr's debut YA novel was launched in 1972. Many people who first saw the book in bookstores were shocked by the sensational title that seemed ripped from the headlines of a newspaper. In fact, for this reason, it was even banned in some schools. In the early 1970s, most Americans were only just beginning to become aware of teenagers' use of drugs. However, young readers recognized themselves in Kerr's well-drawn, believable characters such as Tucker and Dinky. They also saw their parents in both the Hockers (who give lots of money but little attention) and the Woolfs (a kind, supportive couple confronted with Tucker's father's unemployment and his mother's return to college). Parents, librarians, teachers, and teens appreciated the seriousness with which Kerr addressed topics such as drug abuse, overeating, and parental neglect. At the same time, they were tickled by the humorous dialogue and situations in the book.

Critics were also impressed. *Dinky Hocker Shoots Smack!* received positive reviews in almost every library or school-related publication. It was even reviewed by several of the most distinguished American newspapers—a rare occurrence for a new YA author. The *New York Times*, for example, hailed the book as a "superb first novel . . . full of wit and wisdom and an astonishing immediacy that comes from spare [simple], honest writing."[1]

M. E. Kerr was pleased to receive so much attention for her writing. Being reviewed had always been important to her. A success with publishers, readers, and reviewers alike, it seemed as if Kerr had a shining career in store for her as a young adult novelist. In truth, however, Kerr admits that the publication of *Dinky Hocker* was initially a great disappointment.

3 A Young Adult Pioneer

As M. E. Kerr sat down to write her second YA novel, she was thinking that it would also be her last novel for young adults. It wasn't that she didn't enjoy writing stories for and about teens. She had been stunned upon receiving her first check for the hardcover sales of *Dinky Hocker Shoots Smack!* The payment was $2,000—shockingly less than the $15,000 to $20,000 she usually received for writing an adult book. It certainly wasn't enough money to live off.

A New Home

Fortunately, however, the paperback edition of *Dinky Hocker* came out soon after. Sales were strong enough that Kerr happily discovered that what she had initially viewed as a sideline could actually provide her with financial stability. In fact, in 1973, Kerr was able to move out of New York City and settle on nearby Long Island. She purchased a house in East Hampton, a charming 300-year-old seaside town. Since the early twentieth century, East Hampton had been attracting writers and artists as well as wealthy New York families who bought or built elaborate summer homes there.

M. E. Kerr adored her new home. It was a perfect place to write. Nonetheless, one thing she missed was the daily contact she had maintained with other writers in New York. Their discussions about books and writing were important to her. Since the city was fairly close, Kerr began inviting writer friends to visit. However, it was one thing to have lunch with writer colleagues once every few months and quite another to have them staying in her house for an entire weekend. Thinking there had to be another solution, she placed an ad in the local paper advertising a writers' workshop. The enormous response led to the creation of the Ashawagh Writers' Workshop. Kerr ran the weekly meetings, which included writers of all ages and from all backgrounds and professions. The fees they paid went toward a scholarship fund for disadvantaged students. Kerr has been so happy with the workshop that she still continues to operate it. Some of the writers who answered the original ad are still members of the group.

A New Audience

Even though she had been producing adult fiction for twenty years, M. E. Kerr didn't have any trouble switching gears and writing for a younger audience. In fact, in many ways, her former writing experience served her very well. Crafting suspense stories had taught her to write page-turning plots with limited description—perfect for the entertainment requirements of a younger audience. She was a pro at immediately hooking a reader from the opening lines of a novel.

Kerr claims she loves writing for kids because she usually has some important topic she wants to discuss. She feels that, in general, kids are much more open to the notion of change and new ideas than adults who usually have already made up their minds about most subjects.

Over the years, Kerr has written about subjects ranging from dysfunctional families, class and race conflicts, and physical handicaps to homosexuality, AIDS, religious fundamentalism, and suicide. While never preaching or talking down to her readers, Kerr stresses the complexity of these issues and explores various points of view. Showing respect for young people, she never shies away from shocking but realistic truths.

Since *Dinky Hocker Shoots Smack!*, she has published twenty-two books as M. E. Kerr—almost one per year. In the 1990s, she also began to write books for middle school children under the name Mary James. Being one of YA literature's most productive authors has allowed her to constantly attract new readers while satisfying old fans who eagerly await the publication of a new M. E. Kerr book.

The Birth of YA Literature

In the early 1970s, young adult literature was just emerging as a field of its own. Attracted to its possibilities, a fresh crop of writers was dealing with problems that affected young people and which had long been considered taboos. This new openness stemmed from the sweeping social changes that were occurring in the United States during the 1960s. The civil rights movement, the rise of feminism, and protests against the U.S. government's involvement in the Vietnam War were major events throughout the mid- to late

1960s that led to more open attitudes. Women, black Americans, gays, and other "minorities" demanded that their voices be heard. So, for the first time, did young people who took an active part in protests and created a strong youth culture. A result of these new freedoms and this growing emphasis on young people was the birth of YA literature.

Students were tired of studying "classic" novels that in no way mirrored the reality of their lives. Teachers and librarians, excited by the sudden wealth of new YA literature, were quick to fill their classrooms and libraries with these contemporary novels. They were helped by the U.S. government, which, at the time, contributed significant amounts of money to support public and school libraries. This strong demand for YA books attracted many talented writers, including M. E. Kerr. Kerr was one of a handful of pioneers of YA literature who specialized in a type of fiction that came to be known as the problem novel.

4 Problem Novels

M. E. Kerr's past experience with child psychology and her exposure to young people's emotional problems provided her with a great deal of knowledge and sensitivity that quickly made her one of the most popular and critically acclaimed authors of problem novels. In fact, certain novels were very groundbreaking at the time they were published.

Her seventh novel, *Gentlehands* (1978), is an example of a novel that stirred up controversy. The novel's main character and narrator, Buddy Boyle, is a working-class teenager from a small town on Long Island. The summer he turns sixteen, he begins a romance with the fabulously rich and beautiful Skye Pennington. Although

Buddy is fascinated with Skye's world, he is bothered by the fact that he is socially inferior to her. He is suddenly ashamed of his parents, who, in turn, worry that he is becoming a snob.

Buddy's one experience with Skye's social circle is a visit he makes with his mother to the home of his wealthy, cultured Grandpa Trenkle. His mother's father is a German immigrant who has settled near the Boyles in a luxurious beach house. It is here that Buddy takes Skye on a date. Lacking any sophistication of his own, he hopes to impress Skye with his handsome grandfather. In fact, Buddy continues to bring Skye to Grandpa Trenkle's and, over time, he becomes very close to the elderly man. As a result, he is shocked when a local paper publishes a story claiming that Grandpa Trenkle is a Nazi war criminal. Nicknamed Gentle-hands, Trenkle is deemed responsible for the torture and death of many Jews during World War II. The article was written by a Jewish descendant of one of Gentlehands's victims. It exposed the fact that Trenkle's wealth came from the melted-down gold teeth and jewelry of Jews who were killed.

Upon publication, the novel created considerable uproar. Many people were shocked that a villainous Nazi was portrayed in such a sympathetic light. Some people claimed that the novel discriminated against Jews. They argued that the Nazi grandpa was a much more attractive character than the Jewish reporter who tracked him down and exposed him. M. E. Kerr was not surprised by many readers' reactions. In fact, she had hoped to stir people up by illustrating that it is not always possible to recognize evil. Kerr's message—that appearances can be deceiving—apparently registered with both critics and young readers. To date, *Gentlehands* is one of her most popular books.

Another novel that explored a complex issue—this time AIDS (acquired immunodeficiency syndrome)—was *Night Kites* (1986). In this book, seventeen-year-old Erick Rudd, the novel's narrator, begins his senior year with everything going his way. However, life becomes complicated when Erick's older brother and idol, Pete, returns home from New York and reveals two secrets that shock the Rudd family: he is gay and dying of AIDS. Erick and his parents struggle to balance their feelings about homosexuality with their love and concern for Pete. In the meantime, they also have to deal with the hostile reactions of their community once Pete's secret becomes public knowledge.

Kerr wrote this novel at a time when many people still hadn't heard about AIDS. In fact, *Night*

Kites was one of the first YA books written on the subject. Even those who did know about the virus shared many of the biases, fears, and misconceptions of Erick's family, classmates, and neighbors. Kerr herself admits that during the late 1980s, many teachers were wary of the book. When she came to speak at their schools, they asked her in advance not to discuss *Night Kites*. In the 1990s, however, attitudes changed as the AIDS epidemic became so serious that education about the disease was considered essential.

At the time she was writing this book, Kerr never imagined that AIDS would become a worldwide epidemic. She believed that a cure would soon be discovered. Nonetheless, her bravery in dealing with such a controversial issue and of exposing the complex feelings of people confronted with disease and differences won her much acclaim. Noted children's literature critic Anita Silvey, editor of the *Horn Book Magazine* for many years, singled out Kerr as

> . . . one of the few young adult writers who can take a subject that affects teenagers' lives, can say something important to young readers about it, and can craft what is first and foremost a good story, without preaching and without histrionics [theatrical displays of emotion].[1]

41

Kerr tackled the issue of homosexuality once again in 1994 with her novel *Deliver Us from Evie*. In this book, the main character, Evie, is the eighteen-year-old daughter of a Missouri farmer. Evie is a bright, hardworking girl who loves farm work and poetry. She is also a "butch" (a very masculine) lesbian who fights off her mother's efforts to set her up with a young farmer and make her look more feminine. Evie doesn't try to hide her sexual orientation when she begins a romance with the daughter of the richest and most powerful man in the county.

Although Evie has no problem with being a lesbian, her family, her girlfriend's family, and the rest of the conservative rural community are extremely upset by her sexuality. Even Parr, her sixteen-year-old brother and the novel's narrator, feels uneasy. He fears that Evie's relationship with Patsy will result in her leaving the farm, where she is much needed. And he doesn't want his new girlfriend—the daughter of fundamentalist Christians who consider homosexuality a sin—to know of this "shameful" side of his sister.

Although teachers in a few schools were uncomfortable discussing this novel with their students, Kerr received letters from many young girls who thanked her for addressing the issue of lesbianism in such an honest way. Writing for *Booklist*, renowned author and children's literature critic Hazel Rochman praised this "landmark" novel for its sensitive treatment of a complex subject. As Rochman continues,

> We've come a long way from the stories of homosexual love that end in disaster . . . If Kerr's message is more overt [obvious] than usual, it's a complicated message, and she has a lot of fun with it . . . It's a story that challenges stereotypes, not only about love, but also about farmers and families and religion and responsibility—about all our definitions of "normal."[2]

Another complex topic that M. E. Kerr decided to address was war, specifically the United States' role in the Persian Gulf War. In 1991, American soldiers had been sent to Kuwait to fight against Iraqi invaders led by the dictator Saddam Hussein. The scars of this war were still fresh in people's minds when Kerr wrote *Linger* (1993). Kerr proudly claims it is the only YA novel that deals with the Gulf War.

Linger is narrated by sixteen-year-old Gary Peel, whose older brother, Bobby, joins the army and is sent to fight in the Gulf War. The war provokes different reactions among the residents of Gary's small Pennsylvania town. Ned Dunlinger, the wealthy owner of the restaurant where Gary's family works, is proud of America's fighting men abroad and covers the restaurant with U.S. flags and yellow ribbons. Meanwhile, Gary's teacher, Jules Raleigh, protests the war. Gary's account of happenings at home in the United States is interspersed and contrasted with Bobby's journal entries and letters from the Middle East, where he is eventually wounded by friendly fire. Kerr carefully includes a great variety of viewpoints in the novel. However, her message is clear: war is not noble but cruel.

Although critics praised her efforts, some adults viewed her criticism of the war as a lack of patriotism. Kerr recalls that one parent wanted the book removed from a school library. The parent complained that *Linger* presented characters who protested the war in a more positive light than those who supported it. Kerr responded that she had written the book after coming across a newspaper photo of a young soldier who returned from the Gulf War completely disfigured. She had been shocked and outraged when she discovered that his wounds were the result of friendly fire.

Kerr continued this discussion of U.S. roles in foreign wars in a more recent novel. *Slap Your Sides* (2001) tells the tale of Jubal Shoemaker, a

Gay and Lesbian YA Novels

Both *Night Kites* and *Deliver Us from Evie* are considered by many critics as two of the finest examples of a new and rapidly growing literary sub-genre: the gay and lesbian YA novel. Gay characters have been present in novels for teens since the late 1960s—the earliest days of young adult fiction. The first novel to focus on a homosexual relationship was John Donovan's *I'll Get There. It Better Be Worth the Trip* (1969). It told the story of a lonely thirteen-year-old boy who falls in love with his best friend. At the time, Donovan was very brave. Most authors were afraid to tackle the taboo subject of homosexuality. Similarly, most editors were afraid to publish books about homosexuals. In fact, over the next ten years, very few novels with gay themes were published. Among the most notable breakthroughs were Isabelle Holland's *The Man Without a Face* (1970), Sandra Scoppettone's *Trying Hard to Hear You* (1974), Rosa Guy's *Ruby* (1976), and Mary W. Sullivan's *What's This About, Pete?* (1976). During this time, M. E. Kerr also featured openly gay characters in her novels, notably Charlie Gilhooley in *I'll Love You When You're More Like Me* (1977).

Sandra Scoppettone's *Happy Endings Are All Alike* (1978) deals with a teenage love story between two girls. The novel sold poorly and was ignored by most reviewers. A few years later, Nancy Garden's classic lesbian novel, *Annie on My Mind* (1982), was popular with critics and the public. However, it met with resistance from some parents who objected to its presence in school and public libraries and tried to have it banned. To this day, librarians in some parts of the United States are wary about stocking a gay- or lesbian-themed novel for fear of some parents' negative reactions. Out of moral or religious convictions, these people view homosexuality as a sin that shouldn't be talked about, much less read about.

In earlier problem novels with gay characters, homosexuality itself was viewed as a "problem" that had to be dealt with by the gay characters and their friends and family. In these books, a "gay lifestyle" was often accompanied by risks and dangers, ranging from losing one's job to being beat up. Furthermore, few gay relationships survived the conflicts, pressures, and prejudices that surrounded them.

Fortunately, in the 1990s and 2000s, as gays and lesbians became more visible and accepted in American society and culture, homosexuality became less of a "problem" and simply another defining aspect of a person's identity. In *Deliver Us from Evie*, for instance, Evie has no trouble coming to terms with her homosexuality. Instead of depicting her as a troubled victim, most of her scenes in the novel illustrate her (very capably) involved with work on the family farm.

Since the late 1990s, there has been a small explosion of gay and lesbian YA fiction. An average of ten to twelve gay-themed novels are published every year. This is a lot considering that only 130 novels total have been published in this category in the last 100 years, according to Christine Jenkins, a library science professor at the University of Illinois who tracks YA novels with gay and lesbian content. M. E. Kerr has made her own recent contribution to this new harvest of gay YA fiction. In 1997, she published *"Hello," I Lied*, a novel in which the main male character is bisexual.

To Kerr, this growing trend must be satisfying, particularly when she thinks back to the beginning of her writing career. After all, writing under the name Vin Packer, she helped pioneer lesbian fiction when she published her first book, *Spring Fire*, in 1952. At the time, gay and lesbian relationships always had to end tragically or the books wouldn't pass postal inspection (these paperbacks were shipped by mail). When Kerr submitted her finished novel, her publisher made her change the happy ending. Perhaps, for this reason, more than forty years later, Evie and Patsy (from *Deliver Us from Evie*) got to live happily ever after.

young Quaker growing up in a small Pennsylvania town during the mid-1940s. Because Quakers promote pacifism, Jubal is against the war, as is his older brother, Bud. However, Bud's refusal to go to war and his decision to become a CO (conscientious objector) cause problems for the Shoemaker family. Like a boy Kerr remembers from her hometown of Auburn, Bud is the only CO in a town where most young men have been sent to fight in Europe. Those who have stayed behind feel that the Nazis must be defeated at all costs and view Bud's pacifism as cowardly and un-American. In light of the United States' hotly debated roles in Afghanistan and Iraq, this novel— and the tough issues it raises—have proved extremely timely.

5 In Search of Characters

In her critical biography, *Presenting M. E. Kerr*, author Alleen Pace Nilsen points out that getting to know M. E. Kerr the person is, in some ways, more difficult than getting to know other YA authors. A private person, Kerr avoids discussing the details of her personal life. Although she enjoys visiting schools, she rarely does public readings, interviews, or book tours. While reserved in public, Kerr tends to be much more present in her novels than other YA authors.

Whereas various colleagues of hers draw on experiences they have had as parents or teachers, Kerr has never taught school (although she claims being a teacher would have been her next choice of profession if she hadn't become a writer) and has no children of her own. As such, in attempting to make her characters believable, she reaches back to moments and events in her own life.

For instance, there are strong similarities between Flanders Brown, the heroine of *Is That You, Miss Blue?* (1975), and Marijane Meaker when she was a teenager. For high school, both were sent away from small-town homes in New York State to Episcopalian boarding schools in Virginia where they felt like outsiders. At school, both Flanders and Marijane shared rooms with preachers' daughters and girls with physical disabilities. Away from home for the first time, they realized that they are a lot less sophisticated, knowledgeable, and well off than many of the other girls. Moreover, at Charles Hall, Flanders develops a crush on her teacher, the highly intelligent and religiously devout Miss Blue—an occurrence inspired by a crush Marijane had on one of her own teachers at Stuart Hall. In the end, these encounters and experiences are important because they reveal an awareness of differences between individuals. These differences and the conflicts they generate would become a major theme in Kerr's fiction.

Celebrating Differences

Unlike many other YA authors, Kerr doesn't write about jocks or cheerleaders, rebels or class clowns, fashionable cliques or tough gangs. She writes about the kind of young person she was: someone who was confused about life and insecure about herself and the aspects of herself that set her apart from other kids.

For instance, as Kerr was herself, many of the female protagonists are tomboys. Dinky Hocker (from *Dinky Hocker Shoots Smack!*) dresses in her father's old tweed jackets worn over pajama bottoms. In *Little Little* (1981), the character of Cowboy (whose real name is Emily) strolls around like a farm boy who's finished his work in the fields. Then there is Evie Burrman (*Deliver Us from Evie*), who feels uncomfortable in "female stuff" and whose one concession to makeup is a blond streak in her short, slicked-back hair.

When this coincidence was pointed out to M. E. Kerr in a Web discussion group, Kerr was fascinated. She responded by saying, "It's always interesting to me when a reader points out similarities in my fiction I wasn't aware of." She continues, "Of course I know who they [these 'tomboy girls'] all are, just not how many of me I created."[2]

Other teenage protagonists, both male and female, resemble M. E. Kerr in less direct ways. However, all are perceived by themselves, their families, their peers, or their communities as being "different." In her early novels, Kerr's characters are different in fairly common ways: Dinky Hocker is overweight, Flanders Brown (*Is That You, Miss Blue?*, 1975) is asthmatic, Duncan Stein (*If I Love You, Am I Trapped Forever?*, 1973) is Jewish, and Opal Ringer (*What I Really Think of You*, 1982) is poor. Over time, however, Kerr exaggerated these differences by creating characters who were outlandish and even exotic.

In *Little Little*, Sydney Cinnamon is not merely a dwarf; he is an orphaned, hunchbacked, high school dropout who makes a living by dressing up as a cockroach for TV commercials. In *What Became of Her* (2000), Rose Fitch, aside from being poor, lives in a funeral home where she cleans bodies while taking care of her mentally retarded father. Later, as a wealthy widow, she dresses in men's clothing, has a collection of exotic fish, and lives with a life-size leather doll that she treats like a person.

Kerr's characters are rejected, made fun of, and isolated for being poor, unattractive, religious, nonwhite, deformed, gay, or unconventional. When working-class Buddy Boyle steps out of his social milieu to date the wealthy Skye Pennington (*Gentlehands*), he finds himself humiliated when Skye's fashionable friends make fun of his cheap sweater. And in *Little Little*, Sydney Cinnamon, the hunchbacked dwarf, is called everything from an elf to a shrimp cocktail.

However, Kerr also makes sure that her characters draw strength and courage from their differences. Readers with problems of their own can easily relate to these characters. As she admitted in a recent interview: "I tend to write about people who struggle, who try to overcome obstacles, who usually

Literary Heroes

Almost all of Kerr's main characters are serious readers and writers. Like young Marijane Meaker, they while away hours in libraries or curl up with a good book. In fact, Kerr's first novel, *Dinky Hocker Shoots Smack!*, begins with the narrator, Tucker, confessing to be a library-lover and admitting his dream career: to become a librarian. As a teen, Kerr had wanted to study to be a librarian. However, her father was against this idea. He warned that Marijane would never meet a husband enrolling in library sciences, since this was a course traditionally taken only by young women.

Kerr's lonely heroes overcome their tough circumstances, in part, because of their bookishness and literary talents. Poor and friendless, John Fell (hero of the novels *Fell*, *Fell Back*, and *Fell Down*) becomes celebrated at his posh boarding school when he wins a major writing competition. Evie Burrman finds refuge in the love poetry she composes and shares with her brother Parr. In *If I Love You, Am I Trapped Forever?* (1973), Duncan Stein, nicknamed "Doomed," goes from being a loser to a winner when he starts a school newspaper, like Kerr did in college.

In all of Kerr's novels, both male and female characters write journals, poems, notes, newspaper articles, and award-winning essays (many of which are reproduced in the novels). They communicate by letters and by e-mail. Indeed, many of her novels are filled with excerpts from poems and quotes by famous authors. Moreover, through her intellectual characters and the wisest of their teachers, Kerr provides her readers with interesting snippets of information about writers ranging from Socrates and Plato to J. D. Salinger and Robert Cormier.

do, but sometimes not. People who have all the answers and few problems have never interested me, not to write about, not to befriend."[1]

Friendship and Romance

The friendships in Kerr's novels seem to reflect her observation about people who struggle. While most of Kerr's young characters start out lonely, over the course of the novel, they befriend other characters who are as eccentric or unpopular as they are, though in different ways. For example, two principal characters of *Fell Down*, Nels Plummer and Leonard Tralastski, seem to have nothing in common aside from not knowing a soul at their posh new boarding school. While Nels is relaxed, charming, wealthy, and very short, Lenny is tall, brooding, ashamed of his cheap clothes, and insecure about his lack of culture. Their shared status as outsiders brings them together, but their individual differences allow them to act as foils to each other, highlighting each other's strengths and weaknesses in a dramatic manner. These differences also lead to tension and conflict.

This technique of bringing opposites together also characterizes most of the romances in Kerr's novels. Many of Kerr's characters are attracted to partners who are their opposites. Differences can be seductive, but they can lead to conflict, especially if one person tries to submerge his or her differences to please the other—a tendency reflected in the title of Kerr's novel *I'll Love You When You're More Like Me* (1977). A message that is central in all of Kerr's books is that one shouldn't hide one's true individuality to conform to others' expectations. Those who attempt to do so—such as Buddy Boyle with Skye Pennington in *Gentlehands* and Erick Rudd who shields his family and his AIDS-stricken brother from Nicki Marr in *Night Kites*—end up unhappy in love.

In contrast, those who are true to themselves are given happy endings. Such is the case with Evie and Patsy in *Deliver Us from Evie*. Although they come from different socioeconomic backgrounds and differ physically (Evie is masculine, while Patsy is described as feminine), both embrace their homosexuality and their romance succeeds. The same occurs with Little Little and Sydney Cinnamon, the two teenage dwarfs in *Little Little*. While Little Little is a wealthy "p.f." (perfectly formed) dwarf and Sydney is a poor orphan dwarf with a deformity, both are very sure of themselves and assume their differences.

Interestingly, Kerr rarely deals with sex in her novels. Instead, she prefers to explore the more subtle emotional and psychological aspects of love with all its desires, frustrations, and doubts. In

Presenting M. E. Kerr, Alleen Pace Nilsen declares that Kerr "chooses to make her books stand out as different by taking the more challenging route of exploring subtle emotions rather than overt [direct] sexual behavior."[2]

Indeed, aside from romances, almost all of Kerr's novels center around a firm friendship between a young man and a young woman. Perhaps these relationships stem from M. E. Kerr's own teenage experiences with boys. Although she knew she was a lesbian, she truly enjoyed spending time with young men. "In those days you covered your tracks,"[3] she confessed in a posting on her Web site, referring to the difficulty of being openly gay in the 1940s. She goes on to state that teenage sex was generally quite uncommon back then. In the meantime, she truly loved male companionship and her closest friends were male.

Families

In all of her novels, family relationships are important. Kerr believes that adolescence is a time when young people start questioning their relationships with their families as well as their peers. For the most part, the parents in Kerr's novels are a source of not only conflict, but of love and support as well. Never one-dimensional, Kerr's parents are as multilayered as her teens. As the *Horn Book Magazine* critic Mary Kingsbury points out, this is "an obvious strength in the Kerr novels, one that sets them apart from the many contemporary novels nearly devoid of well-developed adult characters."[7] Evie's mother, in *Deliver Us from Evie*, is a good example of a well-rounded character. While she spends much of the novel criticizing Evie for her lack of femininity and pushing her toward marriage with a local farmer, Mrs. Burrman is also the first to admit that Evie is gay. She also protects Evie from Mr. Burrman's anger when Evie spends the night with Patsy. Meanwhile, Evie's father, who has doted on Evie since she was a child and encouraged her tomboy ways, refuses to talk to her once he discovers her sexuality.

With her adult characters, Kerr also uses the dramatic technique of contrasting foils to show that there are many kinds of mothers and fathers. In *Night Kites*, for example, Mr. Rudd is shocked by his son's homosexuality and AIDS, but he ultimately supports and stands by him. The same can't be said for Nicki's father, Mr. Marr, who has gay men thrown out of his hotel and bans his daughter from seeing Erick for fear of her coming into contact with Erick's older brother's disease. Similarly, Dinky's image-conscious, neglectful, wealthy parents are a far cry from Tucker's less-than-perfect but down-to-earth and supportive parents in *Dinky Hocker Shoots Smack!* Ultimately, Kerr's complex portraits of adults encourage her teenage characters and readers to view their parents more realistically and with greater understanding. One of the strengths of Kerr's YA fiction is that it doesn't limit itself to depicting adolescence. With great skill, Kerr weaves together teenage and adult concerns, creating a complex world that reflects real life.

6 A Writer's Life

When M. E. Kerr sits down to write a new novel, the first thing she does is think up the characters' names. She can never actually begin a book until she has named her characters and feels certain that each name suits the fictional creation that is taking shape in her imagination. This attention to names dates back to her childhood, when her father would read aloud the novels of the famous nineteenth-century English author Charles Dickens. She was fascinated by Dickens's colorful names such as Nicholas Nickleby (*Nicholas Nickleby*, 1838), Scrooge (*A Christmas Carol*, 1843), Pip and Estella (*Great Expectations*, 1860), and Sidney Carton and Madame Defarge

(*A Tale of Two Cities*, 1859). The names themselves revealed a great deal about the characters. The descriptive possibilities of a well-chosen name never left her. Sometimes, even once she has begun to write, she is forced to change a name because it no longer seems to suit the character she's created.

The Name Game

Ever since she was young and loved making up pseudonyms for herself, M. E. Kerr has been obsessed with names. She attributes this passion of hers to the fact that she always hated her own first name, Marijane, and her middle name, Agnes. As a novelist, Kerr is always on the lookout for unique names. She has even become a collector of people's old school yearbooks, which she browses through in search of good names.

School visits are another source of interesting names. Kerr enjoys traveling to schools to introduce her books and talk about writing with young people. Whenever she arrives at a school, she always asks students to write their names on index cards and include a question or a request to read something they have written. She does this not only to make contact with individual students, but because it is a good way to stumble onto an interesting name.

She claims to love the variety of unusual and ethnic names of today's students. When she was a child in the 1940s, popular names tended to be conventional Anglo-Saxon ones like her own.

Kerr's earlier novels are sprinkled with memorable, often alliterative names such as Brenda Belle Blossom, Sydney Cinnamon, Caroline Cardmaker, and Wallace Witherspoon. These names reflect their characters' personalities and quickly lodge themselves in readers' memories. Little Little La Belle is such an obvious name for a wealthy "p.f." (perfectly formed) dwarf that it is comical. So is $uzy $lade, whose name is written with dollar signs because she is so rich. The name Buddy Boyle contrasts strongly with that of his rich girlfriend, Skye Pennington. In the opening to the novel, Buddy himself mentions the fact that rich, beautiful girls never have ordinary names like Mary Smith.

Source of Ideas

When Kerr is in the creation stage of her novels, she thinks more in terms of interesting characters faced with complex situations as opposed to plots. As was noted in previous chapters, many of Kerr's story ideas are based on her own teenage experiences. However, as the years have gone by, she has also looked around her for inspiration. She admits to having many teenage friends and is close to her nieces and nephews, all of whom supply her with ideas for stories. So do memories, news reports, and accidental encounters with people whose situations stick in her mind. Eventually, a first line or image comes to her. Once Kerr has the real facts and details planted in her mind, she can let her imagination run with them.

Gentlehands, for example, was based on the experiences of the seventeen-year-old son of one of Kerr's neighbors in East Hampton. One summer, he fell in love for the first time with a wealthy girl whose family had a vacation house on the beach. While he had just received a ten-speed bike, his girl-friend was driving around in a Porsche. Insecure and intimidated by her family and friends, the boy would visit Kerr seeking advice. This real-life romance inspired the tale of Buddy Boyle and Skye Pennington. During the same summer, Kerr happened to be reading a book about the search for Nazis in America. She was fascinated with the story of one Nazi in particular who was incredibly cruel and also very handsome. She wondered how evil could appear in such an attractive package. Weaving the two stories together resulted in *Gentle-hands*, a book that came to her so easily that she wrote the entire novel in only three weeks.

Kerr's most difficult book was the one that followed: *Little Little*. The novel was inspired by seeing the most popular boy in her hometown go away to Harvard and come back to settle down with a lovely wife. The whole town considered them to be an ideal couple until she gave birth to their first daughter: a dwarf. For years Kerr had begun to write a story based on this family, but she always gave up, frustrated.

The biggest problem was making the dwarfs— Little Little La Belle and Sydney Cinnamon—seem real, without insulting them or being politically incorrect. She wanted the problems they faced due to their height to be shown seriously, but she also wished to inject some humor into their story. Moreover, she wanted all teens who felt different to be able to identify with these two lead characters.

Ultimately, she succeeded. The novel, which noted critic Zena Sutherland called "hilarious yet provocative,"[1] is one of Kerr's most widely read and critically acclaimed. As proof of the book's success, Kerr has received various letters from dwarfs praising it (and offering to play the lead roles if it is ever made into a movie). Of her own books, Kerr ranks it among her favorites, not because she considers it her best novel, but because it was the most difficult to write.

Seducing Readers

When Kerr first started out writing YA fiction, she was told by teachers that most girls would read novels told from a boy's point of view, but that the opposite wasn't true. That's why Kerr told the story of Dinky Hocker through the eyes of her friend Tucker Woolf. To date, almost all of her subsequent novels have featured male narrators, even in cases when the story revolves around a main character who is female. When asked if it was difficult for a woman to write from a male perspective, Kerr has joked that when she wrote mysteries, she sometimes told stories from a murderer's perspective and she had no experience killing people.

Although Kerr wants her readers to think about the serious subjects she discusses, she also knows that they want to be entertained. As such, Kerr works hard to ensure that readers become quickly engaged in whatever story she is telling. She even took a class in headline writing for advertisers in order to help her create catchy titles such as *Dinky Hocker Shoots Smack!* and *If I Love You, Am I Trapped Forever?* Thinking about headlines also helps her with the first lines of her novels. For example, in *Gentlehands*, Buddy wonders what his summer would have

"Wait Till You Hear This..."

How does she know if an idea is going to work as a novel? M. E. Kerr has a foolproof method that she learned from her mother, who was a big gossip. As a child, Kerr remembers eavesdropping on Ida Meaker as she called her friends on the telephone. Before launching into a story, her mother would begin by saying: "Wait till you hear this . . ." It was surprising to Kerr how her mother turned everyday occurrences into something exciting. When Kerr has an idea for a story, she asks herself if it could be one of her mother's wait-till-you-hear-this phone calls. If she feels it couldn't be, Kerr searches for another idea.

been like if he had not met Skye Pennington. Such a line immediately hooks readers and contains elements of suspense that make it difficult for readers to put the books down.

Once into the story, Kerr never lets the pace slow down. Her use of first-person narrative gives the story a freshness and directness that allows the narrator's personality to appear without having to use a lot of descriptive detail. Right away, readers identify with teens their own age who share viewpoints and make similar observations. Kerr also relies heavily on direct dialogue to advance the plot. In fact, her books are filled with so many fast and witty exchanges that some pages resemble a film script more than a novel. Kerr is very aware that her books are competing with media such as television, movies, and the Internet. Dialogue allows characters to reveal themselves through their carefully rendered speech patterns, expressions, and vocabulary.

For similar reasons, Kerr is not an author who spends time on descriptive detail. Many of her early novels are set in Cayuta, New York, a fictionalized version of her hometown, Auburn. Later stories often take place in Seaville, a seaside town modeled after East Hampton. However, she takes few pains to describe her settings. Kerr paints her characters' towns, homes, and schools with rapid brushstrokes so as not to interfere with the main characters' interactions with one another.

Although all her main characters attend high school, little of the action actually takes place at school. Classroom scenes and extracurricular activities are rare. Teachers and colleagues are usually relegated to the background. Says Nancy Mercado, an editor at Dial Books for young readers: "There is something so unconventional about her style. Ms. Kerr only puts in the very essential . . . everything else is left out . . . and you don't miss it at all."[2]

Something else Kerr is renowned for as a YA author is her sense of humor. Although many noted writers for teens tackle tough problems with the same sensitivity, few add large doses of comic relief. Indeed, Kerr is an expert at focusing on the weird and surprising moments of everyday life and exaggerating them to the point of absurdity. She also has a love for the eccentric and offbeat.

Not one but two of her main characters, Wallace Witherspoon in *I'll Love You When You're More Like Me* and Rose Fitch in *What Became of Her*, grow up working in funeral homes (as did one of Kerr's teenage boyfriends back in Auburn). Such a setting provides many instances of dark humor and off-key jokes. Kathleen Horning, director of the Cooperative Children's Book Center, summed up Kerr's humorous tone well during an online discussion of M. E. Kerr. "It's something in her voice, just on the edge of sarcasm, but grounded in compassion, the voice of an intelligent, thoughtful teenager. There's also frequently a bit of social satire as well that gives her stories added depth."[3]

M. E. Kerr at Work

Because she goes to bed late, M. E. Kerr likes to sleep in late. Around 3 PM, she goes into her study and works until evening. Then, much later, around midnight, she'll go over what she wrote earlier. Before going to sleep at 2 AM or 3 AM, she'll make notes about what to work on the following day.

When she is at work on a novel, Kerr doesn't talk about her stories with anyone. And she doesn't ask colleagues to look over her manuscripts and share their opinions with her before mailing them to her editor. Instead, she prefers to work alone, keeping each book in its own protected world. Until the manuscript is in her editor's hands, she is afraid to expose her work to the possibility of other people's criticism.

In interviews, Kerr often says that successful writing is based on two activities: constantly reading the books of others and constantly rewriting one's own. When she first began writing YA literature, she read a lot of works by other YA authors in order to remain aware of her competition. Recently, however, she reads mostly adult literature, and lately she reads even more books than she used to—ever since she discovered that just because she starts a book she doesn't actually have to finish it. (Kerr grew up believing that a good reader was obliged to struggle through to a book's end.) A self-described media freak, Kerr claims to read five newspapers a day. She also loves MTV and rock music, both of which help keep her up-to-date with youth culture.

In 1993, she was honored with the distinguished Margaret A. Edwards Award. She was
praised for

> . . . her courage to be different and to address
> tough current issues without compromising and
> with a touch of leavening [lightening] humor,
> [which] has earned her a place in young adult
> literature and in the hearts of teenagers.[4]

Kerr doesn't let such praise go to her head. In
her book of essays about writing, *Blood on My
Forehead* (1998), she displays both modesty and
humor when she talks about some of the reactions
she gets when she visits kids at their schools:

> Certain teachers pass out Author Evaluation
> Sheets among the students and, at my request,
> send the comments on to me. I learn a lot from
> them, and occasionally I'm humbled.

> One of the answers to the question "What did
> you like most about Ms. Kerr's talk?" came from
> a boy named Wallace.

> "Sitting next to Brenda," Wallace wrote.[5]

Interview with
M. E. Kerr

This interview is excerpted from an interview that took place between M. E. Kerr and Teenreads.com writer Audrey Marie Danielson on May 19, 2000.

Prolific author M. E. Kerr joins Teenreads again to talk about her new novel, *What Became of Her*, a book that combines Kerr's poignant fiction with characters inspired by real people. Writing in the voice of a female lead protagonist is unusual for Kerr who spends most of her YA novels in a male voice. Teenreads.com Writer Audrey Marie Danielson asks Kerr about her history of creating mostly male characters, her writing life before YA novels, how she is so well versed in teen culture, and much more in this interview.

AUDREY MARIE DANIELSON: What are the primary issues that you deal with in your novels? Do find yourself returning to similar themes again and again?

M. E. KERR: I tend to write about people who struggle, who try to overcome obstacles, who usually do, but sometimes not. People who have all the answers and few problems have never interested me, not to write about, not to befriend.

AUDREY MARIE DANIELSON: Why did you choose to write books for Young Adults rather than for the adult market?

M. E. KERR: I wrote books for adults long before entering the YA field, mostly mystery books under the name Vin Packer, out of print now. Some were under my own name, Marijane Meaker. YA was a refreshing change, and I prefer writing for kids because they haven't made up their minds yet about life, and are more open to wonder and change than most adults.

AUDREY MARIE DANIELSON: Why do you think it's important to discuss subjects such as child abuse, incest, homosexuality, AIDS, and racism in YA books?

M. E. KERR: I haven't written about incest . . . but whatever the subject is, the story is more important than the issue. I don't decide: now I'll write a book about a child molester, or a homosexual . . . It's a stronger pull than that, usually based on someone I know, or some part of my own life. People interest me more than themes.

AUDREY MARIE DANIELSON: How do you keep up with the latest teenage trends? Do you enjoy their music and all the other elements of the teenage culture?

M. E. KERR: I have many friends who are teens, and I do like the music. But I also was a teen once myself; it's not a foreign country, exactly: teendom. The styles are different from my day, the fads . . . but not the feelings.

AUDREY MARIE DANIELSON: Of all the books you've written as M. E. Kerr and Mary James do you have a personal favorite or favorites?

M. E. KERR: I don't have a favorite book of mine, but *Little Little* was hard to write, and like a child who's hard to raise but then turns out fine, I have a special feeling for that book.

AUDREY MARIE DANIELSON: How emotionally involved do you get with your characters?

M. E. KERR: No, I don't get emotionally involved with my characters, but I do get very involved with them, more intellectually: watching them form, finding the best way to show the readers things about them, making errors and correcting them . . . that sort of thing.

AUDREY MARIE DANIELSON: Who are the authors who influenced you as a child?

M. E. KERR: As a kid I read everything from Nancy Drew mysteries to Charles Dickens novels. I loved the American writers, too, like John Steinbeck, Erskine Caldwell, Sherwood Anderson . . . all the wonderful champions of the underdog who wrote in the 30s and 40s.

AUDREY MARIE DANIELSON: How old were you when you knew that you wanted to be a writer?

M. E. KERR: I can't remember a day when I didn't want to be a writer.

AUDREY MARIE DANIELSON: Who are your favorite YA authors today?

M. E. KERR: There are so many fine YA writers . . . Han Nolan, Robert Cormier, Robert Lipsyte, on and on. I think some of the best writing is in the YA field.

AUDREY MARIE DANIELSON: When you first started writing, how hard was it to get your first novel published?

M. E. KERR: I did not have trouble getting my first book published. I was working as a file clerk for the publisher, so I had access. But that was another time. There was not the media competition then. There were few TV's, no computers, no VCRs. It was a smaller world, far more welcoming to a young writer. I was lucky.

AUDREY MARIE DANIELSON: What is the biggest obstacle that you had to overcome in your writing career and what was your solution in overcoming this?

M. E. KERR: The biggest obstacle was supporting myself writing. I wrote all kinds of things to earn my living until I was able to support myself fully as a novelist. Several times I almost gave up and hunted for a steady job . . . but somehow I stuck with it and it worked. I was a very eager, ambitious young woman; and because I'd gone to the University of

Missouri for journalism, many friends from school came to New York City when I did. We all wanted to be writers. I had a lot of company. We all started off poor and full of hope.

AUDREY MARIE DANIELSON: What is your writing day like?

M. E. KERR: I stay up late, two or three in the morning . . . and sleep late. I eat lunch out by myself or with a friend. I go into my study about 3 PM and work until 6 or 7. Then much later, around midnight, I look over what I wrote and make notes about what I'll do the next day . . . I'm usually working on a novel, so there's never a question about what to write.

AUDREY MARIE DANIELSON: What advice would you give to aspiring authors?

M. E. KERR: I would tell aspiring writers to read. Read, read, read, read . . . Read the kind of books you'd like to write. Study your competition, see how they do it. Go away to college, or to work or whatever. See some of the world away from where you live. Try to join or start a writers' group where everyone shares what they're working on.

AUDREY MARIE DANIELSON: Can you tell us what you're working on now?

M. E. KERR: I'm now writing an adult memoir of the writer Patricia Highsmith, who wrote the book *The Talented Mr. Ripley*.

AUDREY MARIE DANIELSON: Do you get personally involved in the promotion of your books such as lectures, book signings, and bookstore functions? Are you doing any signings for your new book?

M. E. KERR: I do get somewhat involved with promoting my books in that I like to visit schools and talk with the kids. I also go to teachers' conferences, too; and I do telephone hookups with classrooms. But I don't do bookstore appearances, or signings like that. I can't spare the time for that.

Reprinted with permission by Teenreads.com

Timeline

1927 M. E. Kerr is born Marijane Agnes Meaker on May 27, in Auburn, New York.

1943 At sixteen, Kerr is sent to Stuart Hall, a boarding school in Virginia.

1945 Having graduated from high school with low marks, Kerr spends a year at Vermont Junior College.

1946 Kerr attends the University of Missouri, where she majors in English literature.

1949 Upon graduating, Kerr moves to New York City and works at a series of odd jobs while she writes stories.

1951 As "Laura Winston," Kerr publishes her first short story in *Ladies' Home Journal*.

1952 Under the pseudonym Vin Packer, Kerr publishes her first novel, *Spring Fire*.

1958 As "Ann Aldrich," Kerr publishes *We Walk Alone*, the first of five journalistic novels featuring lesbians in New York City.

1964 As "M. J. Meaker," Kerr publishes her first nonfiction book, *Sudden Endings*, a study of famous people who committed suicide.

1972 Writing for the first time under the name of M. E. Kerr, Kerr publishes her first young adult novel, *Dinky Hocker Shoots Smack!*

1973 Kerr moves from New York City to her own house in East Hampton, New York.

1983 Kerr publishes *Me, Me, Me, Me, Me: Not a Novel*, a book of autobiographical stories based on her childhood and adolescence.

1986 Kerr's novel *Night Kites* is one of the first novels to feature a character with AIDS. Following the publication of this book, Kerr begins to openly admit to being a lesbian.

1990 As "Mary James," Kerr publishes *Shoebag*, her first children's book.

1993 Kerr's novel *Linger* is the first and only YA novel to deal with the Gulf War of 1991. In the same year, Kerr is awarded the distinguished Margaret A. Edwards Lifetime Achievement Award for her contributions to young adult literature.

1998 Kerr publishes *Blood on the Forehead: What I Know About Writing*, a book of essays about writing.

1999 Kerr receives the Knickerbocker Lifetime Achievement Award from the New York State Library Association.

2000 Kerr receives a Lifetime Achievement Award from ALAN (Assembly on Literature for Adolescents, National Council of Teachers of English).

2003 Kerr publishes her most recent book to date, *Snakes Don't Miss Their Mothers*.

Selected
Reviews from
School Library
Journal

Deliver Us from Evie
1994

Gr 9 Up—A skilled mechanic and farmer on her family's Missouri spread, Evie Burman, seventeen, has a streak of blond in her slicked-back dark hair, a sign quietly calculated to ward off other people's assumptions—for starters, that she'll marry Cord Whittle, and that she'll help Dad keep the farm going. Evie's story is affectingly told by her younger brother, Parr, who understands as their parents cannot that Evie is falling in love, not with Cord Whittle, but with the daughter of the man who holds the mortgage on their farm. Parr's observations are telling: "You'd say Evie was handsome. You'd say Mom was pretty." Meanwhile, Parr falls for a girl whose fundamentalist family is fearful of gayness, and tension builds slowly until the truth about Evie explodes out of Parr, not just to their parents, but to the whole town. This is first-rate storytelling, with Kerr in absolute control of the narrative. Evie never seems a victim, nor are there villains. With the exception of the rich man who hold the Burrman mortgage, all of the characters are likable. All are survivors. Among the most convincing lesbian characters in young adult fiction, Evie makes a lasting impression, and Parr himself, the loving but conflicted brother, is just as finely drawn and memorable.

Fell Down
1991

Gr 7–12—This third novel about John Fell (*Fell*, 1987, *Fell Back*, 1989, both HarperCollins) opens in the Edwardian Room of the Plaza Hotel. Keats has taken Fell there so she can learn why he walked away from the Gardner School, leaving exams and graduation behind and unfinished. Fell, distraught over the death of his best friend, Dib, in a car accident, needs to make sense of the events that led also to the death of one Lenny Last, a washed-up Vegas comedian/ventriloquist and former Gardner student. By doing so, Fell gets caught up in a twenty-eight-year old mystery. The telling of *Fell Down* is distinctly different from the earlier books: in alternating chapters, the two stories—past and present—are told by Fell and "The Mouth," whose identity is not revealed until the end. This device is jarring at first, but it eventually serves up an intriguing read as the events merge to create a satisfying whole. There is sure to be another book about Fell around the corner, for he returns to the newly coed Gardner School and Sevens House to find April, the sister of the love-of-his-life, Delia. A must purchase for libraries in which the other two books about Fell are popular.

Little Little
1981

Gr 7 Up—Teenage Little Little La Belle—dwarf daughter of the town of La Belle's leading family—has led a hothouse life with her pushy mother, forcibly overprotective father and jock sister. Sydney Cinnamon, a hunchback dwarf abandoned at birth, is a self-made local celebrity appearing as the Roach, symbol of Palmer Pest Control. P.P.C's upcoming merger with the Japanese-owned Twinkle Traps factory, based in La Belle, brings the two together. Hired by Twinkle's Mr. Hiroyuki, Sydney's the surprise entertainment at Little Little's exclusive— "perfectly formed" only—coming-out party. Also on the guest list is the elder La Belle's hoped-for son-in-law, TV preacher Little Lion—none other than huckster Knox Lionel, a.k.a. Opportunity Knox, Sydney's pragmatic mentor ("make sure your little ass goes first class") from their "Leprechaun Village" days. It takes a satirist of no small rank to poke pointed fun at the boosterism and pecking order of a TAD (The American Diminutives) convention without missing its members' painful vulnerability and isolation in an outsize world. This Kerr manages with only one misstep. But if the factory owner's son Mock Hiroyuki ("Riddre Riddre") skates too close to the kind of Asian caricature once favored by Jerry Lewis, the rest is bizarrely real and refreshingly funny.

Me, Me, Me, Me, Me
1983

Gr 7 Up—Ingenious and innovative. A series of landmark episodes from Kerr's childhood, teens and first adult years are related with her wit and special brand of narrative skill. Taking place during World War II and immediately after, this is, first and foremost, a tale of growing up in the days when parents laid down rules for behavior: permission for dating, approval of friendships, laws for etiquette; gratuitous advice on everything was a parental right. Using her father's caustic journal as a counterpoint to her own view of events, she portrays those years wryly. To each episode is appended postscriptive commentary showing characters recast into Kerr's popular YA novels, and, sometimes, those same characters updated with irony. Instead of giving examples of "how to write," Kerr uses this poignant autobiography as both example and lesson. A tour de force, it will be enjoyed not only by young fans of her novels but by a wide range of older audiences of would-be writers and once-upon-a-time kids. That's almost everybody.

Night Kites
1986

Gr 7 Up—Kerr's skill at characterization does not fail her in this love/family story. Erick is comfortable with his senior crowd, delighted with his girl Dill and his best friend Jack. But Jack falls for Nikki, an insecure fashion-plate who wants only what she can't have. Erick tries to steer Jack clear of such a troublemaker, so Nikki sets her sights on him next. Complicating his guilt for betraying Jack and Dill by seeing Nikki is Erick's misery over learning that his beloved older brother Pete has AIDS. Thus, the horrified family finds out about Pete's imminent death at the same time they find out about his life style. The conflict between the Rudds' former feelings about homosexuality and their love for their son is clear, even in the face of the hostility that Pete's illness causes within their community. The book abounds with endings: the old dog that Pete had slyly named Oscar Wilde must be euthanized; Nikki dumps Erick, just as she discarded all the other boys she captivated . . .

Selected reviews from *School Library Journal* reproduced with permission from *School Library Journal* copyright © 1981, 1983, 1986, 1991, 1994 by Cahners Business Information, a division of Reed Elsevier, Inc.

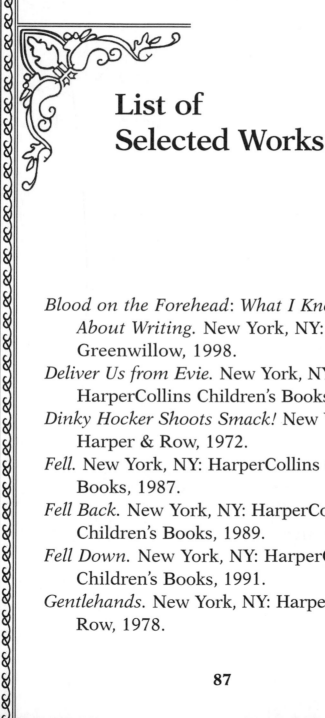

List of
Selected Works

Blood on the Forehead: *What I Know About Writing*. New York, NY: Greenwillow, 1998.

Deliver Us from Evie. New York, NY: HarperCollins Children's Books, 1994.

Dinky Hocker Shoots Smack! New York, NY: Harper & Row, 1972.

Fell. New York, NY: HarperCollins Children's Books, 1987.

Fell Back. New York, NY: HarperCollins Children's Books, 1989.

Fell Down. New York, NY: HarperCollins Children's Books, 1991.

Gentlehands. New York, NY: Harper & Row, 1978.

"Hello," I Lied. New York, NY: Greenwillow, 1997.

Him She Loves? New York, NY: Harper & Row, 1984.

If I Love You, Am I Trapped Forever? New York, NY: Harper & Row, 1973.

I'll Love You When You're More Like Me. New York, NY: Harper & Row, 1977.

I Stay Near You. New York, NY: Harper & Row, 1985.

Is That You, Miss Blue? New York, NY: Harper & Row, 1975.

Linger. New York, NY: HarperCollins Children's Books, 1993.

Little Little. New York, NY: Harper & Row, 1981.

Me, Me, Me, Me, Me: Not a Novel. New York, NY: Harper & Row, 1983.

Night Kites. New York, NY: HarperCollins Children's Books, 1986.

Slap Your Sides. New York, NY: HarperCollins Children's Books, 2001.

Snakes Don't Miss Their Mothers. New York, NY: HarperCollins Children's Books, 2003.

The Son of Somebody Famous. New York, NY: Harper & Row, 1974.

What Became of Her. New York, NY:
    Greenwillow, 2000.
What I Really Think of You. New York, NY:
    Greenwillow, 1982.

List of Selected Awards

ALAN (Assembly on Literature for Adolescents, National Council of Teachers of English) Award for Significant Contribution to Adolescent Literature, 2000

The New York State Library Association's Knickerbocker Lifetime Achievement Award, 1999

Margaret Alexander Edwards Award, 1993

***Deliver Us from Evie* (1994)**

American Library Association (ALA) Best Books for Young Adult Readers (1995)

Booklist Editors' Choice (1994)

The *Horn Book Magazine* Fanfare Honor List (1995)

Dinky Hocker Shoots Smack! (1972)

American Library Association (ALA) Notable
Children's Book (1972)

School Library Journal (SLJ) Best of the Best in
Young Adult Literature (1970–1983)

School Library Journal (SLJ) Best Children's
Books of 1972

Fell (1987)

American Library Association (ALA) Best Book
for Young Adults (1987)

Booklist Editor's Choice (1987)

Fell Back (1989)

Finalist, Edgar Allan Poe Award, Best Young
Adult Mystery (1990)

Fell Down (1991)

Booklist Editors' Choice (1991)

Gentlehands (1978)

American Library Association (ALA) Best Books
for Young Adult Readers (1978)

American Library Association (ALA) Best of the
Best Books (1966–1992)

American Library Association (ALA) Notable
Children's Book (1978)

New York Times Best Children's Books of 1978

School Library Journal (SLJ) Best Children's
    Books of 1978

If I Love You, Am I Trapped Forever? (1973)
New York Times Best Children's Books of 1973

I'll Love You When You're More Like Me (1977)
School Library Journal (SLJ) Best Children's
    Books of 1977

I Stay Near You (1985)
American Library Association (ALA) Best Books
    for Young Adults (1985)

Is That You, Miss Blue? (1975)
American Library Association (ALA) Notable
    Children's Books (1975)
American Library Association (ALA) Best Books
    for Young Adults (1975)
New York Times Outstanding Children's Books
    of 1975

Little Little (1981)
American Library Association (ALA) Notable
    Children's Books (1981)
American Library Association (ALA) Best Books
    for Young Adults (1981)
School Library Journal (SLJ) Best Children's
    Books of 1981

Winner, Golden Kite Award, Society of Children's Book Writers (1981)

Me, Me, Me, Me, Me: Not a Novel **(1983)**
American Library Association (ALA) Best Books for Young Adults (1983)

Night Kites **(1986)**
American Library Association (ALA) Best of the Best Books (1966-1980)
American Library Association (ALA) Best Books for Young Adults (1986)
Booklist Editors' Choice (1987)

The Son of Someone Famous **(1974)**
School Library Journal (SLJ) Best Children's Books of 1975
School Library Journal (SLJ) Best of the Best (1966–1978)

Slap Your Sides **(2001)**
Booklist, one of 10 Best Books About Religion (2002)

What I Really Think of You **(1982)**
School Library Journal (SLJ) Best Children's Books of 1982

Glossary

AIDS (acquired immunodeficiency syndrome) A disease caused by HIV that attacks the immune system, leaving a person vulnerable to infections and illnesses.

alliteration The repetition of sounds (usually consonants) in two or more words.

anthropology The study of human beings and their origins and cultures.

civil rights movement A movement that took place during the 1960s in the United States in which many discriminated groups of people—primarily African Americans—fought for the equal rights that they had been guaranteed under the Constitution.

Communist A believer in a political system in which all goods and property are owned and shared equally by all people.

concession Recognition or admission of someone else's argument or viewpoint.

conform To agree with and copy standard customs or forms of behavior.

conscientious objector (CO) A person who refuses to bear arms or fight a war due to moral or religious beliefs.

conservative People or beliefs that are traditional; cautious of change.

controversy A dispute in which strongly held opposing viewpoints come into conflict.

devout Strongly religious.

disgruntled Discontented, ill-humored.

do-gooder Someone who is extremely committed to helping others (even those who don't want help).

eccentric Strange, offbeat, or different from the norm.

ecstatic Extremely happy, thrilled, or excited; to be elated.

Episcopalian A member of the Episcopalian Protestant Church.

foil Someone or something that serves as a contrast to another.

friendly fire Discharge of a military weapon that hurts or kills an ally.

fundamentalist A strong believer in a set of strict traditional (usually religious) values, often while rejecting other beliefs.

grotesque Fantastically weird, absurd, or ugly.

Hemingway, Ernest Famous American writer and novelist (*A Farewell to Arms*, *The Old Man and the Sea*) who committed suicide at the age of sixty-one in 1961.

Hinton, S. E. Famous young adult author, Susan Eloise, from Tulsa, Oklahoma, who wrote one of the first important works of young adult realistic fiction, *The Outsiders*, in 1967, when she was seventeen years old.

histrionics Theatrical display of emotion.

ideological Concerned with certain ideas, theories, or concepts.

inevitable Unavoidable, inescapable.

inquisitive To be curious.

intimidating To be frightening, bullying.

leaven To lighten, as in the tone of a story.

liberal An open-minded person who objects to traditional ideas and customs and supports individuals' freedoms and rights.

Margaret A. Edwards Award A distinguished award given every year to a YA author for his or her entire body of work by the Young Adult Library Services Association.

martini A cocktail made with gin, vermouth, and an olive.

Monroe, Marilyn The famous blond Hollywood movie star of the 1950s who committed suicide at the age of thirty-six in 1962.

Nazi A member of the German Fascist Party that controlled Germany under Adolf Hitler between 1933 and 1945, and was responsible for the death of more than 6 million Jews in European concentration camps.

outlandish Very strange, wild, out of the ordinary.

pacifism Opposition to war or violence as a means of solving problems.

paradox Contradiction; something that is different from what it seems or is expected to be.

Peck, Richard Young adult author of realistic fiction whose 1976 book *Are You in the House Alone?* was one of the first books for teenagers to address the often-taboo issue of rape.

Plato The famous Greek philosopher who lived from 428 to 347 BC.

protagonist A main character.

pseudonym A pen name; an invented name used by an author to disguise his or her real identity.

psychoanalyst A doctor who treats emotional and mental problems by having the patient examine his or her dreams and childhood experiences.

psychology The study of mental behavior.

reciprocated Returned, shared, shown by two people or sides.

rifts Conflicts, divisions.

Salinger, J. D. Famous twentieth-century American author of *The Catcher in the Rye*.

smack Slang for the drug heroin.

sociology The study of human society and its institutions and organizations.

Socrates The famous Greek philosopher who lived between 470 and 399 BC.

sorority A traditional college sisterhood or social club of women students.

tabloid A newspaper that specializes in scandalous, often untrue, or exaggerated news.

taboo Something prohibited because it shocks or frightens traditional society.

tomboy A female (usually a young girl or a teenage girl) who tends to behave—be it in terms of speech, interests, language, gestures, or dress—in a way that is usually considered to be masculine.

uproar Excitement, commotion.

ventriloquist A person who performs with a dummy, providing the dummy's voice without moving his or her lips.

vitality Liveliness.

wary To be uncomfortable, uneasy, cautious.

Zindel, Paul Distinguished playwright whose first young adult novel, *The Pigman* (1968), is a classic in the young adult fiction genre.

For More Information

Web Sites

Due to the changing nature of Internet links, the Rosen Publishing Group, Inc., has developed an online list of Web sites related to the subject of this book. This site is updated regularly. Please use this link to access the list:

http://www.rosenlinks.com/lab/meke

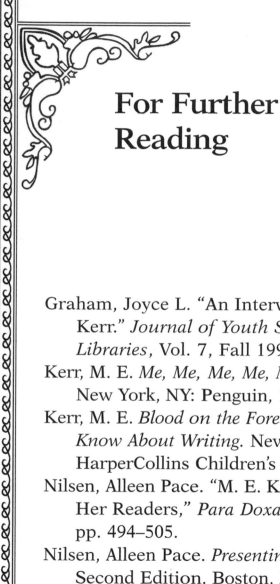

For Further Reading

Graham, Joyce L. "An Interview with M. E. Kerr." *Journal of Youth Services in Libraries*, Vol. 7, Fall 1993, pp. 26–31.

Kerr, M. E. *Me, Me, Me, Me, Me: Not a Novel.* New York, NY: Penguin, 1984.

Kerr, M. E. *Blood on the Forehead: What I Know About Writing.* New York, NY: HarperCollins Children's Books, 1998.

Nilsen, Alleen Pace. "M. E. Kerr: Awakening Her Readers," *Para Doxa*, Vol. 2, 1996, pp. 494–505.

Nilsen, Alleen Pace. *Presenting M. E. Kerr.* Second Edition. Boston, MA: Twayne Publishers, 1997.

Spencer, Pam. *What Do Young Adults Read Next? A Reader's Guide to Fiction for Young Adults.* Farmington Hills, MI: Gale Group, 1994.

Sutton, Roger. "A Conversation with M. E. Kerr." *School Library Journal*, Vol. 39, June 1993, pp. 24–29.

Bibliography

Bradford, Richard. "The Nazi Legacy: Undoing History." Review of *Gentlehands*, *New York Times Book Review*, April 30, 1978, p. 30.

Carson, Dale. "Smack." Review of *Dinky Hocker Shoots Smack!*, *New York Times Book Review*, February 11, 1973, p. 8.

Cooperative Children's Book Center (CCBC) at the School of Education, University of Wisconsin-Madison Web site. "Discussion of M. E. Kerr's Books." Published June 2002. Retrieved June 2004 (http://www.soemadison.wisc.edu/ccbc-net/jun2002.text).

Kerr, M. E. *Blood on the Forehead: What I Know About Writing.* New York, NY: HarperCollins Children's Books, 1998.

Kerr, M. E. *The Books of Fell.* New York, NY: HarperTrophy, 2001.

Kerr, M. E. *Deliver Us from Evie.* New York, NY: HarperTrophy, 1995.

Kerr, M. E. *Gentlehands.* New York, NY: HarperTrophy, 1990.

Kerr, M. E. *Little Little.* New York, NY: HarperTrophy, 1991.

Kerr, M. E. *Night Kites.* New York, NY: HarperTrophy, 1987.

Kerr, M. E. *What Became of Her?* New York, NY: HarperTrophy, 2002.

M. E. Kerr and Mary James Official Web site. Retrieved June 2004 (http://www.mekerr.com/).

Mona Kerby's Author's Corner: M. E. Kerr. Retrieved July 2004 (http://www.carr.org/mae/kerr/kerr.htm).

Kingsbury, Mary. "The Why of People: The Novels of M. E. Kerr." *The Horn Book Magazine*, Vol. LIII, No. 3, June 1977, pp. 288–295. Cited in *Children's Literature Review*, Vol. 29. Detroit, MI: Gale Research, p. 132.

Nilsen, Alleen Pace. *Presenting M. E. Kerr.* New York, NY: Dell, 1986.

Rochman, Hazel. Review of *Deliver Us from Evie. Booklist*, Vol. 91, September 15, 1994, p. 125.

Silvey, Anita. Review of *Night Kites.* The *Horn Book Magazine*, Vol. 62, September/October 1986, p. 597.

Sutherland, Zena. Review of *Little Little. Bulletin of the Center for Children's Books*, Vol. 34, No. 8, April 1981, pp. 153–154.

TeenReads.com. "Author Profile: M. E. Kerr." Retrieved July 2004 (http://www.teenreads.com/authors/au-kerr-me.asp).

Vandergrift, Kay E. "Learning About M. E. Kerr." Retrieved July 2004 (http://www.scils.rutgers.edu/~kvander/kerr.html).

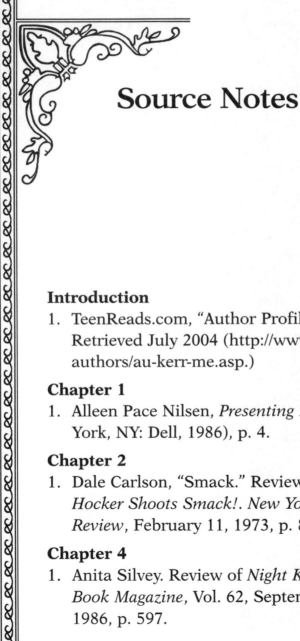

Source Notes

Introduction
1. TeenReads.com, "Author Profile: M. E. Kerr." Retrieved July 2004 (http://www.teenreads.com/authors/au-kerr-me.asp.)

Chapter 1
1. Alleen Pace Nilsen, *Presenting M. E. Kerr* (New York, NY: Dell, 1986), p. 4.

Chapter 2
1. Dale Carlson, "Smack." Review of *Dinky Hocker Shoots Smack!*. *New York Times Book Review*, February 11, 1973, p. 8.

Chapter 4
1. Anita Silvey. Review of *Night Kites*. *The Horn Book Magazine*, Vol. 62, September/October 1986, p. 597.

2. Hazel Rochman. Review of *Deliver Us from Evie*. *Booklist*, Vol. 91, September 15, 1994, p. 125.

Chapter 5

1. M. E. Kerr in an interview during an online discussion about her work. Posted on CCBC Web site (Cooperative Children's Book Center at the School of Education, University of Wisconsin-Madison), June 20, 2002. Retrieved June 2004 (http://ccbc.education.wisc.edu/ ccbc-net/jun2002.text).
2. M. E. Kerr interview with Teenreads.com., published May 19, 2002. Retrieved July 2004 (http://www.teenreads.com/authors/au-kerr-me.asp).
3. Alleen Pace Nilsen, *Presenting M. E. Kerr* (New York, NY: Dell, 1986), p. 109.
4. M. E. Kerr. "Re: Ann Aldrich/Vin Packer???" Posted on M. E. Kerr Message Board, July 14, 2000. M. E. Kerr Web site. Retrieved July 2004 (http://www.mekerr.com).
5. Mary Kingsbury. "The Why of People: The Novels of M. E. Kerr." *The Horn Book Magazine*, Vol. LIII, No. 3, June 1977, pp. 288–295. Cited in *Children's Literature Review*, Vol. 29, Detroit, MI: Gale Research, p. 132.

Chapter 6

1. Zena Sutherland. Review of *Little Little*. *Bulletin of the Center for Children's Books*, Vol. 34, No. 8.

2. Nancy Mercado, editor of *Dial Books for Young Readers*, in an online discussion about M. E. Kerr's work. Posted June 6, 2002 on CCBC Web site (Cooperative Children's Book Center at the School of Education, University of Wisconsin-Madison). Retrieved June 2004 (http://ccbc.education.wisc.edu/ ccbc-net/jun2002.text).

3. Kathleen Horning, host of an online discussion about M. E. Kerr's work. Posted June 10, 2002 on CCBC Web site, June 20, 2002. Retrieved June 2004 (http://ccbc.education.wisc.edu/ccbc-net/jun2002.text).

4. Citation from Margaret A. Edwards Award. Reprinted on Teenreads.com, "Author profile: M. E. Kerr." Retrieved July 2003 (http://www.teenreads.com/authors/au-kerr-me.asp).

5. M. E. Kerr. *Blood on the Forehead: What I Know About Writing*, p. 74. (New York, NY: Greenwillow, 1998).

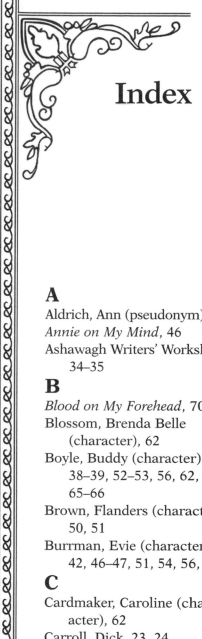

Index

About the Author

Albert Spring is a writer with an MA in literature and civilization.

Photo Credits

Cover, p. 2 © Zoe Kamitses.

Designer: Tahara Anderson; **Editor:** Joann Jovinelly
Photo Researcher: Hillary Arnold